Yellow Umbrella Books are published by Red Brick Learning
7825 Telegraph Road, Bloomington, Minnesota 55438
http://www.redbricklearning.com

Library of Congress Cataloging-in-Publication Data
Ring, Susan.
    [Big or small.Spanish]
    ¿Grande o chiquito?/por Susan Ring.
    p. cm.
    Includes index.
    Summary: "Simple text and photos show that animals can be big or small and
can be sorted into groups by their size"—Provided by publisher.
        ISBN-13: 978-0-7368-6001-7 (hardcover)
        ISBN-10: 0-7368-6001-0 (hardcover)
        ISBN 0-7368-3078-2 (softcover)
[For CIP information, please refer to http:www.loc.gov]

Written by Susan Ring
Developed by Raindrop Publishing

Editorial Director: Mary Lindeen
Editor: Jennifer VanVoorst
Photo Researcher: Wanda Winch
Adapted Translations: Gloria Ramos
Spanish Language Consultants: Jesús Cervantes, Anita Constantino
Conversion Assistants: Jenny Marks, Laura Manthe

Photo Credits
Cover: Grant Woodrow/Image Ideas, Inc; Title Page: Photo 24/Brand X Pictures;
Page 4: Deirdre Barton/Capstone Press; Page 6: Deirdre Barton/Capstone Press;
Page 8: Richard T. Nowitz/Corbis; Page 10: Bill Hilton Jr./Hilton Pond Center;
Page 12: David Pinquoch/Alaska Good Time Charters; Page 14: Melissa Rickers/
USDA Forest Service/Chippewa National Forest; Page 16: Ralf Schmode

1 2 3 4 5 6 11 10 09 08 07 06

¿Grande o chiquito?

por Susan Ring

Yellow Umbrella Books
for early readers

Este caballo es grande.

Este caballo es chiquito.

Este pájaro es grande.

Este pájaro es chiquito.

Este pez es grande.

Este pez es chiquito.

¿Quién es grande?
¿Quién es chiquito?

Índice

caballo, 5, 7

chiquito, 7, 11, 15, 17

este, 5, 7, 9, 11, 13, 15

grande, 5, 9, 13, 17

pájaro, 9, 11

pez, 13, 15